the forever thing

JAPJOT SINGH

Front cover image: Japjot Singh.

Book design: Japjot Singh.

Printed by Notion Press, in India.

Written with Love ♥

First edition 2025.

for you ♥

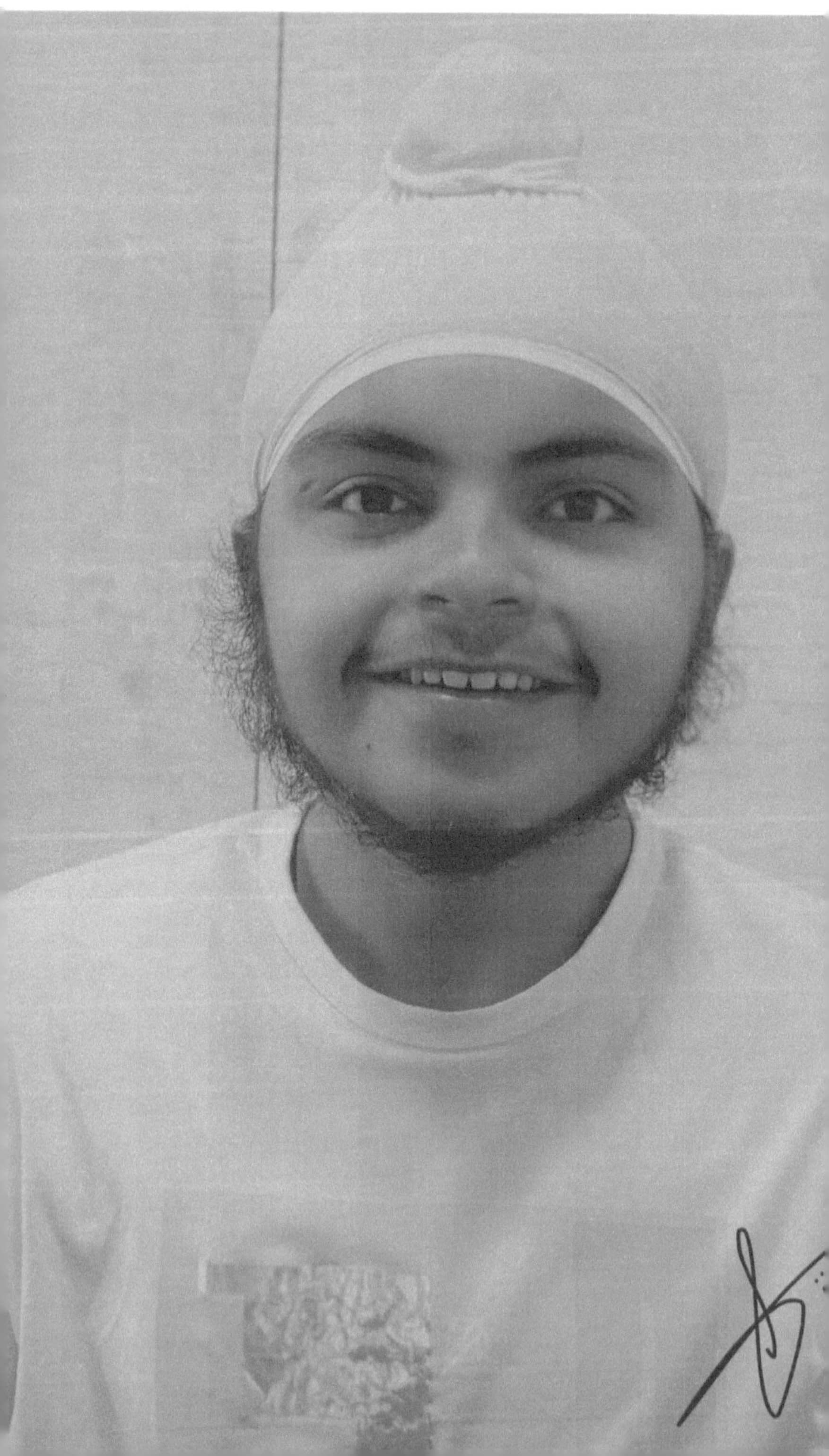

the forever thing

Japjot Singh is a poet and storyteller loved by his close ones. This spring, he became 16 years old, writing more pieces every day he wakes up. He lives with his family in Ranchi, writing some words of art, which makes him feel home.

If you like reading this book, you could appreciate my art at @japjots.ingh on Instagram. I would love to hear from you!

I am very grateful to you to be reading this book, thank you so much cuties to support me,

Love you :)

I wrote it
at times
I felt
love is true
-Japjot
XOXO!

I deleted, typed and typed again and wrote this book for love, with love and by love.

the forever thing

'The mirror reflects only her image, yet still dazzles and confounds my eyes.'

-    *Mirza Ghalib*

the forever thing

This book will make you feel love a little more than
yesterday<3.

Dear Reader,

I started writing this book few months ago *for you* to cherish the love in life.

No matter what they say, I wrote my heart out, in the form of poetry and proses. As you read, I unbox my heart into these pages. I am deeply honoured that you chose my book among so many others.

Enjoy~

Japjot Singh

the forever thing

I dug a part of me

and my soul speaks of you

my heart smiles

and my soul speaks of you.

the forever thing

I read once

that the cells in our body

replace themselves every seven years

does that mean

I have loved you

with every part of me-

twice?

the forever thing

the rainbow adores

the colourful you

dancing merrily in the streets

as we play holi

and the sky's hues fade

vanishing-

just as my heart beats.

Japjot Singh

the forever thing

I do not need

a fairytale ending

just you

on a quiet morning

pouring me coffee.

the forever thing

falling in love with you

felt like sitting on a swing-

effortless,

exciting,

and somehow,

I never want to stop.

the forever thing

you called me *beautiful*

on a day

I could not even

look in the mirror

I think that's

what love is

the forever thing

could we crash back to the time we met?

as I sleep, dreaming

the art of

falling in love again and again.

the forever thing

you say you love her

do you understand her?

did you ask her how is she?

do you really know her?

people love with heart, you should love her with your mind too.

the forever thing

your love feels like a handwritten note-

something I seem to have-

simple, thoughtful and something I'll keep *forever.*

Japjot Singh

the forever thing

Somewhere, there's a receipt from the café in the middle of the city, where we laughed for hours and hours. Those hours were so fast I could not even think. It proved that *love can cost nothing and still feel priceless.*

Japjot Singh
13

the forever thing

everything's so fast

could you slow it down-

some moments that I be with her.

Japjot Singh
14

the forever thing

it is not

that

I was not loved before

but the warmth of you

on my cold shoulders felt

more precious.

Japjot Singh
15

the forever thing

not all magic is loud

some of it just walks in

smiles and stays.

Japjot Singh
16

the forever thing

no one stayed

but you did

what more could i ask for?

i don't have a diary

but i have you

could i just tell you

every bit of mine?

and you smile like you know me

what more could i ask for?

the forever thing

the way she looked at me

a dream within a dream

i wait for the day

when again we meet.

Japjot Singh
18

the forever thing

Japjot Singh
19

the forever thing

'you write so beautifully' she said

could we write us into forever?

Japjot Singh

the forever thing

the palace shines with the queen

as stars shine in my soul

i'm full of *you*

as we write stories

like happy souls

who found each other

of an eternity.

Japjot Singh
21

the forever thing

i peep from the back of the tree

seeing flowers touch you

in awe

to see you bloom.

Japjot Singh
22

the forever thing

the rain touched my skin

and for a second

it felt like you.

Japjot Singh

23

the forever thing

it only covers one of us

but you tilt it slightly,

so i stay dry

you thought i wouldn't notice?

Japjot Singh
24

the forever thing

i will

i will stay,

long enough

for my heart to stop waiting.

Japjot Singh
25

the forever thing

how will i forget you?

my heart never forgets the path

to your heart.

Japjot Singh
26

the forever thing

love will not trick you,

it will not leave you waiting

for at train that never comes.

love will sit beside you,

patient, even when the storm

pulls the roof away.

Japjot Singh
27

the forever thing

somewhere, the ocean kisses the shore

somewhere, the wind carries a laugh that will never be forgotten.

and somewhere-

even if you can't feel it yet-

happiness is making its way to you.

Japjot Singh
28

the forever thing

i don't want us to be

a garden of

withering flowers

so every morning

I wake up

watering it with

trust, love and sincerity

the forever thing

i'm not tired

i just want to see you smile

and if you are

my arms give a warm hug too

Japjot Singh

the forever thing

you never write 'I love you'

on a note or text

but every week

i find my favourite snack

on the grocery list-

Japjot Singh

the forever thing

I'm glad

that i am not understood

just by a stranger

but you were a stranger too

right?

Japjot Singh
32

the forever thing

I catch people

reading flowers in the letters

given with love

who couldn't catch time with

their love

strange right?

Japjot Singh
33

the forever thing

don't think there's no love

it is there in every leaf, every flower, in every droplet

as the cloud showers

maybe in the people you don't know

maybe in the people we call ours

35

Love is not finding someone who completes you, but someone who makes you forget you were ever incomplete.

the forever thing

i told the moon

about you

and she stayed up all night

just to listen.

Japjot Singh

36

the forever thing

i used to dream of love

like fireworks

then you came along,

now it feels like a sunrise

the forever thing

you are the paper

i write poetry on

-- the only one i express my feelings to.

Japjot Singh
38

the forever thing

so many dead flowers weep on the streets,

could you touch them with love,

and make them alive?

Japjot Singh
39

the forever thing

she has a rare quality-

her innocence

no one could have more than her.

Japjot Singh
40

the forever thing

i don't want to learn anything

but magic

which makes me breathe of you.

I still carry my wired earphones rather than my air pods, just to be beside you - listening you and the tunes you like.

Japjot Singh

the forever thing

"why do you love me?"

"it is easy to be me in front of you without thinking

of what the people say, that makes me love you"

I feared to be unloved

but now I love to the fullest

because one day

I would be

one of the stars

some of the sand

forgetting the stories of who I am.

Japjot Singh

the forever thing

they see your scars and bruises

but i see you are perfect

as you effortlessly love.

Japjot Singh
45

the forever thing

can I have the secrets?

your eyes tell

I don't mind

if they tell our forever.

One day, someone will make you realise who you are and replaces your overthinking nights with ones that have talks which makes you feel lighter and *holds your heart.* Someone who makes you realise *what love really is!*

the forever thing

i've never been this happy

it seems like

butterflies enter my soul

with you and love

running in my veins.

YOU'RE THE ENOUGH

I NEED

AND THE PEACE

I WANT.

the forever thing

i know you hesitate to love

but sometimes

it doesn't only heal you

but gives you another life.

the forever thing

your heart is a piece of art

that someone adores

don't waste it feeling for

someone who doesn't care

the forever thing

'what is special about love?'

'it will find you eventually.'

the forever thing

you gifted me a thought

that all I did is worth it

that I am more than the person

they thought I was

you gifted me hope

the hope that I should go on

to be me

the hope that I am doing

the right thing

along the right path.

BE WATER MY FRIEND,

DRENCH OTHERS WITH LOVE.

Japjot Singh
54

I don't feel lonely

as I wake up in the morning

birds chirp and

you bring spring

to my heart.

Japjot Singh

the forever thing

will you be my forever?

will you be my reason to laugh?

a part of my soul

my other half?

be mine

from the first

till the infinity we last?

Japjot Singh

the forever thing

your voice feels like

a door left open—

I step in and I am home.

the forever thing

the way sunflowers wait

for the presence of sunlight

the way I pass from

that bench in the park

where my soul resides

won't I miss you for the time

you are not here

love the way I lie.

Japjot Singh
58

the forever thing

I really want to go those miles

to meet you again

for I had been searching for you~

true love

IT'S HER EYES,

THEY NEVER LIE.

the forever thing

dear you,

this year hasn't been just another year. I've been loving me more these years, the way my mobile phone dings at 11:59 and i see your message wishing me *happy birthday*, i go into my world of joy and happiness.

-   8.03.2025

the forever thing

dear diary,

this morning i'm at a sweet shop, *with her,* where the confectioner offers us round and sweet *jalebis* and we take small bites and enjoy it!

those little delicacies and laughs we share have neither left my bones nor soul!

those who touch our hearts, leave memories in our souls forever.

Japjot Singh
62

DON'T OVERTHINK,

YOU DESERVE TO BE LOVED, LOVE.

the forever thing

Love is what stays with you forever!

don't cry for the people who leave you but be grateful for the ones who stand for you and be with you.

Japjot Singh

the forever thing

don't wait

tell them how you feel

how you have a space,

a space in your heart for them

tell them

how they mend your heart

a heart which now beats for them

tell them how you feel

before you regret.

Japjot Singh

the forever thing

can i tangle my soul to your hair?

whom wind flirts with

where no one else looked for love.

Japjot Singh

66

the forever thing

will you come?

come again

and hug me

come again

and talk to me

the way we used to

if you go away for a while?

Japjot Singh

the forever thing

you're not asking for too much

you're asking the wrong hearts.

Japjot Singh
68

the forever thing

you healed me

without touching my wounds-

just by being kind

when I wasn't.

the forever thing

I hope you find

a kind of love

that doesn't need to be chased,

only cherished.

some wounds don't close

with time—

they close

with love.

the forever thing

we never said forever—

but you made every moment

feel like it.

Japjot Singh

the forever thing

she loved me like

I was poetry—

and not everyone

knows how to read that.

the forever thing

I love spring

of how the flowers

make love to each other.

Japjot Singh
74

the forever thing

you just held my hand

while I grew roots again.

and that was enough—

you were enough.

the forever thing

we didn't fall in love

we walked into it—

hands brushing,

souls nodding.

like "oh,

there you are."

Japjot Singh
76

you told me

you loved my smile,

so I started wearing it

more often—

not only for you

but for me too.

the forever thing

"I love her and that's the beginning and end of everything"

-   *F. Scott Fitzgerald*

Japjot Singh
78

the forever thing

If I were the moon

I'd shine just for you,

following softly whatever you do.

and when you're asleep,

I'd whisper so low,

"I love you much more than I ever show."

-    THE MOONLIGHT CONFESSION.

the forever thing

I burn in the colour of you.

the forever thing

I see stars in your eyes

every time our paths cross each other.

Japjot Singh

81

the forever thing

This night I stood before the sky as the moon stares at me and I see the shooting star after a while; the one which listened my wish. The wish of living of living an eternity with you without knowing you in the first place. *I'm glad I loved you and wished for a forever, god wrote for me.*

One day I see the world collapsing, where I see every one running for their lives, while I sit in the corner as you hold my soul and I hold yours as I live every day and every moment with you seeing the forever that we hold.

Japjot Singh

the forever thing

Japjot Singh
84

THE ~~END.~~

TILL THE FOREVER.

the forever thing

Japjot Singh
86

THANK YOU

FOR READING.

the forever thing

Japjot Singh
88

www.ingramcontent.com/pod-product-compliance
Lightning Source LLC
Chambersburg PA
CBHW020452160726
47991CB00007B/2617